Scaling Up - Beginner's Guide To Scaling Your Business

Economies of Scale

Knowing the right steps for your business startup

©2019, James King

Published by Expertengruppe

Scaling Up

Beginner's Guide To Scaling Your Business

Economies of Scale

Knowing the right steps for your business startup

Published by Expertengruppe

TABLE OF CONTENTS

ABOUT THE AUTHOR

James King is a successfull business consultant, who lives with his wife and two daughters in New York city. Even though he mostly consults global companies, his passion is to enable startup or long existing small-scale enterprises in becoming more successfull.

He knwos from innumerable years of experience, that with the right mindset, the right tools and the right business foundation, every tiny business can be turned into an extremely successfull and profitable high-scale company.

Since he knows, that most small-scale businesses do not have the financial power or maybe even the courage to hire a successfull and efficient consultant, he started to write affordable beginner's guides for everyone. His dream is, that every entrepreneur, who is willing and ready to bring the neccessary effort, can acquire the knowledge that is needed without overextending himself.

With his guide books everyone – regardless the education level – is able to make a difference in ones business.

FOREWORD

Congratulations! You made an excellent decision by resolving to scale your business. And in addition, you determined to buy this beginner's guide to reach your goals. Thereby you actually made two excellent decisions.

To own a business is not an easy job. To run the business profitably is even more difficult and to scale it successfully is master dicipline. The decision you made, will be the most challenging and stressfull situation, you have ever been into. However, it also offers opportunities you never imagined before.

Before reading the next chapters, you should know, what you can expect from this guide. If you are looking for short cuts or the ultimative magic formular to turn your business into a $1 billion idea, you will be dissatisfied. You will not find any of these on the next pages.

In contrast, if you are looking for explanations, what business scalability is, what you can do and what the risks and opportunities look like, you will be pleased with what you find. After reading this beginner's guide, you will know exactly where to start and what steps you have to take. However, I need to add, that this guide does not replace the complex and intensive guidance of an scaling consultant. Nevertheless, it will be the perfect fundation for your scaling plans and will prepare you at the best possible rate for any further consultation or counselling.

Are you ready to invest not only the next 2 or 3 hours into the success of your business, but the next weeks or months? Are you ready to give your very best and even more?

Then you made the right decision and are now ready to read the next pages.

I wish you all the very best and the success you wish to achieve. If you want it and if you are willing to follow the advises you find in this guide, you will be able to achieve even the highest goals and even more. Go for it!

CHAPTER 1

WHAT IS SCALING?

All of us have heard the buzzword phrase 'scaling your business', but like so many other buzzwords, we only have a vague or fuzzy notion about exactly what it means and since everyone else seems to already know what it means, we're afraid to appear ignorant and ask.

In its generic sense, scalability refers to how well a given system performs, when transplanted into an environment, where significantly greater demands are placed upon it.

BUSINESS SCALABILITY

Granted, that Merriam-Webster definition doesn't really clear things up much, so let's take a look at what scalability means in actual practice for businesses.

A company that has the capability of scaling up can manage its own growth when the time comes, because it has the infrastructure in place to do so.

That means it has the appropriate management, the IT infrastructure, clearly documented business policies and procedures, and the employee resources to handle a much greater volume of business.

Since that is precisely the objective, which most businesses aim at, having a scalable business would seem to be a highly desirable thing.

Generally speaking, scale refers to the size of any operation, and this is true in business as much as any other application.

But there's more to it than that in business, because if a business grows its revenue by increasing its operating cost at the same rate or higher, that is not a business that scales well to the new situation — and it's not a business that will sustain profitability.

By contrast, a business which increases revenue significantly while keeping operating costs the same or minimally higher, scales extremely well.

DIFFERENCE BETWEEN SCALING AND GROWTH

Growing, in a business sense, simply means that your company is adding resources or infrastructure to handle increased demand, at a cost, which is more or less equivalent to the level of increased revenue coming in.

Growth in this model is strictly a measure of greater volume, not of profitability, and certainly not of scaling.

In contrast with that model, scaling occurs, when much greater revenues are pouring in, without you incurring a similar increased level of cost — which means profits should soar.

An example of great scaling would be the business, which adds a large number of new customers, but does not have to bring on hordes of new employees to handle the increase in customers.

MAKING YOUR BUSINESS SCALABLE

One of the very best ways of making your business scalable is to identify those parts of it, which can be reproduced at a very rapid rate, without generating increased costs.

As an example, once a designer/developer has produced a good video game, all subsequent production of the game incurs very little cost, with each game selling for vastly more than it cost to produce it. This is the very essence of scalability.

At its core, this example is an efficiency of mass production, but the same principle can apply to other aspects of your business.

Shipping products might be another prime candidate for achieving efficiencies of scale, perhaps shipping to a centralized distribution centre rather than drop shipping directly to retailers.

Another great way to achieve scalability with your business is to find ways to automate certain processes that currently require human intervention.

Once the automated process has been setup and becomes functional, tremendous efficiencies can be gained, because the slow and tedious process, which required human operation, can be replaced by a quicker, repeatable process ,which has value to a customer.

For business executives of small companies, here are some important perspectives to keep in mind, when looking for scaling opportunities:

- **Embrace standardization**

Don't get bogged down with some ephemeral notion, that you're protecting the entrepreneurial spirit of your company, or that standardizing processes will smother creativity throughout the organization. In fact, it can work just the opposite by standardizing some processes, you may free up yourself or other employees enough to enjoy greater creative freedom in your business.

• Define your true market identity

It's essential that you understand your company's role or position in the overall market, and that you don't doom your company to mediocrity, because you lack the vision to see it in a greater role. Whatever the size of your company, evaluate your position with respect to rivals, identify opportunities when they arise, be aware of threats, and prioritize tasks which can help to achieve scalability.

• Ensure that you have the capacity to be scalable

In order to build for sustainable growth, you need to assemble an organization, that can achieve and maintain that growth. This should be done well in advance of the actual growth, so you have time to build in the necessary capacity to handle that increase, without having the outrageous expenditures, that would result if you were forced to suddenly install capacity.

• Setup a flow of recurring revenue

Leverage your products, your processes, the social media even yourself, if you're a consultant to establish a flow of recurring revenue, so that you're not tied to the business every second of your life. Often this means adding services or products which add value to your main offering, but which involve little or no additional effort on your part.

SHOULD YOU STRIVE FOR SCALABILITY IN YOUR BUSINESS?

There's no easy answer. You either want to scale, or you don't.

Being scalable helps a small business become a big business without incurring the ballooning costs, that might be associated with simple growth. If you choose not to strive for scalability, you can still experience the kind of incremental growth, that comes from simultaneous increases of revenue and cost.

Something to consider about incremental growth however, is what your competitors are doing—are they also content to grow incrementally, or are they scaling their businesses to experience the kind of margin that can only come from efficiencies gained through replication?

When greater revenues actually result in greater profits, and are not simply absorbed by burgeoning costs, that is what makes a company truly scalable.

CAN YOUR BUSINESS SCALE?

I am not talking about dry skin here. What I am talking about is does your business have capability beyond what you do personally? Is your business more than just you?

Have you built a business that can easily grow? This is a challenge for the one or two-person business. If all or most of the sales of the business are based on the effort of the owner, then your business does not have scale, as of yet.

How can you change this? The approach would be to look at expanding your products, your services or your geographic reach beyond what you can do on your own. If you are running one store, consider opening another. Tim Horton's started with one! Can you develop products from the services you offer, so that you increase your revenue? Brain storm around what products you might be able to sell, and consider selling digitally. Can you create reports, checklists or books?

How much income can your business make, if the founder is not involved? We are all looking for passive income, income you can earn in your pajamas. If you make your money by selling your time, as many of us do, then you only have so much time to sell and you can likely only get so much for each hour. In order to grow your business, you have to get beyond selling your time. This is an area where your website will help. Is your website just a brochure for your business? Can you change, that so that your website can sell products for you, and deliver these products all on its own?

What if you had more people's time to sell? If you are able to obtain more work than you can do personally, it is time to hire more employees.

You can be more profitable if you can hire people to do some of the work that you do and this will free up some of your time to do more profitable work.

Can you picture yourself with more employees? If not, why not? Is it possible that what is holding your business back from growth is your own limiting beliefs? Maybe you could scale your business by visualization, which is picturing yourself actually doing it. Imagine your business with 10 more employees or a number of new locations. What would you need to do to make that happen?

If your business is the size that you are comfortable with, then you do not care if it scales, enjoy things just the way they are.

CHAPTER 2

HOW TO SCALE YOUR BUSINESS?

Here's your tip for client attraction, getting more clients, making more money, multiplying your business.

It's about how to scale your business. The way to make a lot more money in your business, more money than you're making now, is to add more value to even more people's lives. And when you do that, you make more money.

It's very simple but it's not always easy. It's common sense you make more money by working with more people and you do that by adding more value.

If you were to think about how can you massively increase your income, if we were to look at your income now and looking for a five times multiplication, five times what you're making now, you would be working with at least five times more people than you're working with now.

The key is looking at your existing business models and see are you working one-to-one right now, hours for dollars? Is your income capped at how many clients you can work with?

If so, you are in a classic Leverage Lucy or Leverage Larry business model. This is where you cannot make more money in your business, because you are trapped into that one paradigm. The key for you to make more money in your business and affect more people's lives, is to change your business model and to look at how you could scale, what you're already doing, so that you can work with so many more people.

Your assignment for the week: How can you offer what you currently offer your clients in a much more scalable business model? Really think about your business model and say, "Okay, how can I scale what I'm currently doing, so that clients still get great results, but I can work with so many more clients?"

Your second question, which is part of your assignment for this week, is to ask yourself, "If I had 100 clients show up tomorrow, brand new clients show up tomorrow, how would I change how I do business to accommodate all of them?"

Maybe you're working with 20 or 30 clients now but imaging, that you had to take on starting tomorrow 100 more clients. What would you need to do to your business model, to how you deliver your information, or your services, so that you could accommodate all these 100 clients. And perhaps for you, you're already doing that, maybe it's 1,000 more people, that you need to imagine.

Really think about those business models. Look to stretch how you think about how you deliver your products and services, to be able to make a lot more money and service a lot more clients.

So thought-provoking thought for the week and I want you to really sit down and noodle this out, write in your journal and look around in either your industry or other industries and look at how other people are scaling their businesses and see what you can model. Just this alone can have you add another zero to your income within the next year.

And I have one more question for you:

Are core values really necessary to scale your business?

What do you think? I recently had the privilege of working with a company that is wildly successful by anyone's standard. Even in this economy, it's growing rapidly, has a culture, that attracts the best talent, is winning award after award in its industry, and has a CEO, who was named local business leader of the year.

However, after meeting with several of the company's key leaders and employees, it occurred to me, that although they had some very clear short-term objectives and were driving the company towards iconic levels of short-term success, the core values, or what I call the SOUL, and ultimately the long-term success, of the company was in danger of being compromised, due, ironically, to its hyper-growth.

When I say SOUL, I'm not talking about the "soul" that is drenched in marketing jargon and marched out to the employees and the public as a feel-good statement, then hung around the office. Did Enron have a soul or a feel-good mission? Did Bernard Madoff's company have a soul or a feel-good mission? Enron's 4 values (Integrity, Communication, Respect, Excellence) were chiseled in marble in the main lobby, but had very little to do with the real values of the organization.

Most companies have 3 basic components: 1) a skeleton, 2) a central nervous system and 3) a SOUL.

1. The skeleton is the organizational structure of the company and tells the

story of how the organization functions. It is very difficult for a company to have the skeleton of a starfish yet perform like a cheetah. Sadly, many companies think they have the skeleton of a cheetah but in reality, they have the skeleton of a rake (one dominant leader with a bunch of people reporting to that individual).

2. The central nervous system includes the systems that create consistent and predictable outcomes for a company. As the saying goes, if you do not design the systems, they will design themselves, often very poorly.

3. The SOUL of a company includes the invisible but very real NON-NEGOTIABLE vision, core values, and goals put upon it daily by the actions, behaviors and

passions of the people, who created and work at the company. The SOUL of a company is both the most significant way for leaders and their team to positively influence the bottom line AND truly make a significant contribution toward making the world a better place...if done authentically.

Simply put, the SOUL of a company is what happens when no one is looking.

WHY DOES YOUR COMPANY NEED A SOUL?

Having been an athlete (some would say "competitive junkie") my entire life, I have come to recognize one thing that makes a sports team uniquely focused and ultimately prepared to win...no matter what, is the same thing that makes companies uniquely focused and ultimately prepared to win...no matter what.

That "thing" is the NON-NEGOTIABLE shared vision, values and goals. The SOUL consistently inspires you and your team toward the right behaviours and anchors you and your team during challenging times. When "corporate tsunamis" strike and they will, you need that anchor to be REAL, to be CLEAR and most importantly, to reflect the DNA of you and your team.

If you pull an "Enron" and have what I call a "SOUL HOLE" (meaning you say one thing and do another). You and your team will no doubt be measured by your actions, and the next stop on that journey is hypocrisy, doubt, fear and cynicism overtaking the corporate culture.

PASSION...YOUR SOUL HAS GOTTA HAVE IT!

There is a dizzying amount of books, articles, blogs etc. about how to come up with your vision and values statement. Quite simply, your vision and values have got to reflect the passion of you and your team. Each word has got to have personal significance to you and your team. NOT what you want it to be, not what you think will feel good to the customers and your employees, but what you ARE NOT willing to negotiate on, EVER! Write your vision, values and goals so they reflect, who you and your team really are, sprinkle your personalities on top and serve it up for your employees, customers, partners, etc to enjoy!

The SOUL of your company should be simple, should be memorable and should drive the right behaviour.

KEEPING THE SOUL ALIVE

If your vision and values are not in some form or fashion at the forefront of everything you do, every meeting you have, every new employee interview you conduct, every decision you make, then you run the very real risk during growth or simply with the passing of time of having the SOUL of your company fade and in extreme cases (e.g. Enron) die.

DO NOT BE A COWARD, BE A LEADER

If your vision and values are REAL, AUTHENTIC and drive your team's DAILY behaviours, congratulations, you are one of the elite. My guess is, although you may experience difficulties from time to time, your organization thrives amidst any crisis it may encounter.

If your vision and values statements are feel good statements, that rarely get discussed and do not reflect the REAL values of you, your team and your company, then do not be afraid to ask for forgiveness from your team and employees and embark on a journey to develop the values and mission, that inspire you and your team. Or if your vision and values have lost their meaning and significance during rapid growth or over time, do not beat yourself up; this is actually a warning sign of your SUCCESS!

Instead, use this opportunity to pull your team back together and breathe life back into your vision and values or maybe adjust accordingly to reflect what is REAL and AUTHENTIC about you, your team and your company.

And let me add one last thing:

I HOPE YOU HAVE THE COURAGE TO MAKE YOUR COMPANY AND THE WORLD A BETTER PLACE... HAPPY SOUL SEARCHING!

CHAPTER 3

BUSINESS FUNDING WILL SCALE YOUR BUSINESS

Most businesses think that business funding is something that you need, when your business is short on cash or times are hard. A lot of businesses go out looking for business funding, when the business is not good. The time to get business funding is not, when your business is doing horrible or you are strapped for cash.

If your business is doing great, there is no better time to go out and get business funding. Why?

1) It's easier to qualify

2) You can get better rates and terms

3) It's easier to grow your revenues with a capital infusion

4) It's easy to utilize the simple formulas that we have in here to scale your growth.

DON'T WAIT FOR THINGS TO GO BAD; IF YOU ARE DOING GOOD - BUSINESS FUNDING CAN SCALE YOUR BUSINESS TO THE NEXT LEVEL.

This is how you can determine, if business funding can help your business grow. There are 5 simple steps, which will show you the value of business funding.

STEP 1

WHAT DO YOU NEED TO GROW YOUR BUSINESS?

While this may sound like a stupid question, it is a very important question.

The FIRST STEP you need to take is determining, what your business needs to grow sales. Most businesses need one or more of the following:

- Inventory and More Products

- Expanding Existing Line of Products

- Adding Additional Services

- Marketing and Advertising

- Sales People or Personnel

- Machinery, Equipment, Software or Hardware

- Expanding into other Territories or Adding Another Location.

STEP 2

HOW MUCH MONEY DO YOU NEED TO ACHIEVE THAT?

How much money do you need to achieve that? Again, another simple question and it may sound stupid. But you need to start off with basic questions.

How much would you like to invest into your business or how much do you need to grow your business?

$10,000, $20,000, $40,000, $50,000, $100,000 +

STEP 3

WHERE WILL THE COME FROM?

There are only three forms of cash that flow into a business:

- REVENUES FROM SALES

- INVESTMENT DOLLARS

- DEBT: A LOAN OR LOANS

Where will the money come from to help your business grow?

If you have an existing business and you want to invest in your business, you either sell more or you have great close out balances and have enough reserves to re-invest. If you plan on selling more; most sales and marketing strategies require some sort of cash infusion. If that is not the case, you only have two options: an investor or a loan.

STEP 4

If you had the amount of money you need to do what you want in your business - there are two key questions: If you know the answers to these two basic questions; you will know immediately, how to increase your sales fast.

1. HOW MUCH MONEY WILL YOU MAKE WITH THAT MONEY?

In technical financial terms: what will be the ROI (Return on Investment)?

2. IN WHAT TIME FRAME WILL YOU MAKE THAT MONEY BACK?

In what time frame will you achieve the anticipated or projected ROI (Return on Investment)?

EXAMPLE (CASE STUDY): (Simple Version)

If someone gave you $100,000 - what would you do and how would that impact your business.

Example:

I (YOUR NAME) would take $100,000 and allocate that money into marketing and increase personnel. (NEED AND WANT)

I (YOUR NAME) would take $100,000 and make 50% return in 5 months. The equivalent of 10% return per month...

Based on this information, you are clear on how you would use the money, what type of return you would make and in what time frame.

The next step; is to determine if you...:

- ... can increase sales to $100,000 and have the extra money to do this.

- ... obtained an investor, how much would they want? Most investors will either charge you anywhere from 10% to 30% in interest or they will want 20% to 50% of net earnings. You have to figure out the cost of capital versus your return.

- ... obtain a loan, the interest rate may range from 7% to 30%. You need to factor in the cost of capital versus your return.

EXAMPLE (CASE STUDY) - Crunching Numbers:

For Existing and Operational Businesses

Food Distributors of America currently generate $50,000 per month on an average. At the end of the month they close out $5,000 positive which is about 10% net. Currently, their cost of inventory is $20,000. This means every month they purchase $20,000 to make $50,000 Gross. The question you need to address is: How much are my costs to generate gross earnings? Once you know that, you know how much you need to increase gross earnings by 10%, 30%, or even 100%. In this example, we can increase earnings by 100% by making a capital infusion of $20,000.

We know that $20,000 generates $50,000 per month. We know that $20,000 and $50,000 of gross sales generates $5,000 per month net;

which is 10%. They want more inventory because they have prospective buyers.

Conclusions:

- An additional $20,000 would generate an additional $50,000 in gross sales; increasing earnings to $100,000. This is a 100% increase in gross sales.

- An additional $20,000 would generate an additional $5,000 in net margins; increasing earnings by another 10% monthly = 20% monthly.

- If this business can do this every single month, they would increase net earnings by 100% monthly.

Not all businesses can do this. Businesses that carry inventory have an easier time achieving this.

Businesses that sell every day; such as restaurants, hair salons, and anyone who sells consumer products; have an easier time achieving this.

Seasonal businesses can also achieve these types of returns.

STEP 5

CALCULATING COST OF CAPITAL VERSUS RETURN ON INVESTMENT (ROI)

If you don't have the extra money; you will need an investor or some sort of business funding or a loan.

There is nothing wrong with taking on investors or a loan. Most successful businesses have grown with capital infusion. Think of this way. Would the New York Stock Exchange or would the Chicago Board of Trade exists if businesses did not take on investors or debt? All businesses on major stock and debt exchanges have investors or debt.

How do you calculate ROI and Cost of Capital? Easy as 1, 2, 3:

Let's assume you are able to obtain a loan for $50,000 to invest in your business. You project that you will make 5% return per month for the next 5 months = 25% return. Let's assume you get a loan with a 12% annual rate = the same as 1% per month.

5% per month (your return) minus 1% = 4% your new return

4% x 5 months = 20% (after cost of capital).

The interest rate on a loan is important. However, if you know how to make a Return on Investment with a loan you will WIN in the end. More important, this is known as OPM (Other People's Money).

CHAPTER 4

BUILD A SUSTAINABLE, DURABLE, SCALABLE AND MORE PROFITABLE BUSINESS

Businesses are born and businesses die every day. Unfortunately, the death rate is increasing and now exceeds the birth rate. This has obviously been caused by the change in the economy. Unfortunately, with small businesses being so vital to the economy, it is also a cause for the continued recession! It's a vicious cycle, but one that can be stopped...

In The E-Myth Revisited (Michael Gerber) published in 1995, Michael Gerber reported that 80% of businesses fail in the first 5 years of trading, and that 80% of those that survive the first five years don't make it past their 10th birthday. Meaning only 4% of new businesses will celebrate their 10th anniversary.

The Office of National Statistics in the UK publish statistics on the "births and deaths" of UK businesses every year. The key statistics from this report are:

- The number of business closing their doors rose by 20,000 (7.4 per cent) to 297,000 for the year between 2009 and 2010

- The number of businesses started remained broadly flat with a small decrease of 1,000 (0.4 per cent)

- For the second consecutive year businesses that stopped trading outnumbered those that started, resulting in a 1.8% drop in the number of active businesses

The data also provides information on the survival rates of businesses.

From this we can see that around 40% of all businesses started in 2005 were still trading in 2010. Somewhat higher than the 20% suggested in the E-Myth.

While there is no data for 10-year survival, modelling the data you can predict that 17% of businesses started in 2005 should see their 10th birthday.

However, the numbers also suggest a decline in survival rates since 2008 as you might expect given the economic conditions. As a result, the average life expectancy for a new business has dropped from 5 years for businesses opened in

2005 to a predicted 4 years for businesses started in 2010.

This is considerably better than the 3 years suggested by the survival rates quoted in the E-Myth. This may mean that things overall are better than they were in 1995. Or it may mean that businesses are more durable in the UK than they have ever been in the US. Or both...

Regardless, if the aim of business is to generate long-term profitable enterprise for individuals and their employees, then the absolute numbers don't matter too much. Most business owners don't start a business expecting it to be there for only four to five years on average.

What to do about it?

While the economy is accelerating the closure of businesses, one of the main underlying causes for the majority of business failures is that most business owners never manage to build a fully systematised business.

Research shows that while the majority of business owners know they need to systematise their business, almost 99% of business owners have been unable to do so. It isn't their fault. No one has ever shown them how to do it.

The business remains for the most part in the head of the owner and so the business cannot function without them. Over time this grinds the owner down until they've had enough and close their doors, never realising the dreams they had, when they opened for business in the first place. Even worse, without business systems in place, it cannot adapt in a declining economy.

Writing systems isn't difficult and yet most businesses don't achieve it. There are many reasons:

- It doesn't seem like profitable work, so it isn't a priority...

- It isn't a very exciting/interesting work, so it's being delayed over and over again...

- It isn't something the owner is good at, so he/she tries to bypass it...

- There are too many distractions from customers, employees, suppliers, etc.

And yet when it is achieved it can and does result in sustainable, durable, scalable and more profitable businesses. So it must be worthwhile putting time aside to start.

WHAT TO CONSIDER WHEN SCALING YOUR BUSINESS

What You Should Keep in Mind When Deciding to Grow Your Business

Regardless of your background in business or what you are offering consumers, beginning a new business is a very risky venture. Statistics show that almost 90 percent of all start-ups fail, and of those 90 percent, roughly three out of four companies failed because they decided to scale up too quickly or too soon. While this may seem like a bleak outlook, the good news is that premature business scaling is completely preventable. Here are some things to keep in mind when scaling your business model.

> ➤ **Consider the State of Your Industry Over the Next Few Years**

The state of your industry has a lot more to do with your business's success than you may believe. Before scaling your business model, consider what the state of the industry may be over the next three, five, or even ten years. Will the industry be able to support the growth of your business? Will you be able to see some profit before the product or service you are offering becomes obsolete? These, among others, are important questions you need to ask yourself before beginning your business growth.

➢ **Make Sure Every Aspect of Your Business is Scalable**

Many small business owners believe that scaling their business is as simple as acquiring more customers and more sales while still using their same business operations. It is important to keep in mind that true scaling usually involves several overhauls of both your business's internal and external operations. Do you have recruitment processes in place to hire more employees to support the demand? Will the technology your business currently uses support a higher workload of increased transactions, accounts, and customers? Scaling your business is more than just selling more of what you are offering.

> ## Think About Your Businesses Culture

When you scale your business, you will often have to hire more employees in order to support the larger operation.

Many small business owners are used to working in small groups, usually less than ten employees, and often do not understand how the business culture and dynamic will change with a larger group of employees working together toward a common goal. When your business begins to grow, focusing on your company's culture will become very important.

Some questions you may want to consider include: "What is your company's culture now?" "What kind of culture do you want your business to have?" "How will you focus on, manage, and grow the company culture you desire?" By documenting best practices and guidelines from others, it will be possible to grow and nurture a culture that will work for your business as well as helping to formalize your strategic ideals, company mission, and other aspects of your growing business.

➢ Keep Short Term and Long Term Goals in Balance

An important part of beginning and sustaining growth is making sure your goals are in balance. Investing in new technology, and/or a new business infrastructure is a short term goal, that can help to lead to longer term growth. But, working toward a long term goal will likely put the shorter term goals on hold. It is important to keep the long term impacts to your business. The short term achievements toward traction is vital for business growth and can often be more of an art than a science.

SUCCESS STORY BY ENTERPRENEUR

KEEP PROCESSES AS SIMPLE AS POSSIBLE

Successful business leaders are often so successfully, because they learn how to be good at simplifying things. They take the complex and make it less complex. This philosophy and approach to business is used in everything from product launches to developing workflows.

Part of the success of Apple under the watch of Steve Jobs was born from his ability to remove things, that were overly complicated. He was notorious for cancelling projects he viewed as extraneous.

Complexity sucks time. It requires more meetings, more explanation, more refined communication with the customer, more people in the workflow, and more cogs in the machine.

Complexity slows businesses down and inhibits growth.

"As businesses grow and scale, the key dynamic that slows progress and, at the extreme, impairs a business, is the creeping effect of complexity," says Arnab Mishra, President and COO of Transera.

"Complexity rears its head as products evolve, organizations grow, and business strategies change. CEOs of growing companies need to be aware of the impacts of growing complexity, and take actions to continuously simplify the operations and strategy of the organization."

"CEOs that are most effective in reducing complexity tend to have a clear and well-communicated vision of the business' goals, an ability to lead employees towards that vision, and a willingness to change course when it becomes clear that certain strategies are not providing the required results."

Keeping your processes simple makes it easy to stay engaged with the people who are the greatest component of your growth and success — your customers.

"Simplicity is really important," says Dan Horan, CEO of Five Acre Farms. "It's got to be simple, and sometimes to make something simple you have to really, really study everything about it. It might turn out to be complex, but you have to present it simply, particularly when it comes to people: when people buy something, they don't want a lecture."

FOCUS ON DELIGHTING YOUR CUSTOMERS

While customer acquisition is important in any business, you need to focus on the customers you have. Customer perceptions can make or break a business. If you deliver quality experiences, products, and service, and you make every effort to delight your customers, then they'll sing your praises.

In a study from Nielsen on advertising, media, and peer recommendations, it was discovered that 92% of consumers around the world trust earned media, such as personal recommendations and consumer opinions from friends and family, above all other forms of advertising.

When you delight your customers, and they share that delight, your business will grow. That's the mind set of Five Guys and they've held that position since their launch in 1986.

"We figure our best salesman is our customer," says Jerry Murrell, CEO of Five Guys. "Treat that person right, he'll walk out the door and sell for you. From the beginning, I wanted people to know that we put all our money into the food. That's why the decor is so simple – red and white tiles. We don't spend our money on decor. Or on guys in chicken suits. But we'll go overboard on food."

Delighting your customers doesn't have to be a time-intensive operation and you don't have to completely restructure your business model. You just need to operate in a way that anticipates their needs and stays with them beyond the point, where they make that first purchase.

STAY TUNED IN TO YOUR BUSINESS

As you grow your business, one of your goals should be hiring smart, talented people to handle various tasks. As a business owner, you can't be involved in everything, so it's important to delegate and let other, better-suited people handle the work.

But that doesn't mean you should step back and tune out. Just because it's being handled, doesn't mean you're not involved.

In an interview with Business Insider, host of the TV show Bar Rescue, Jon Taffer, spoke about a hard lesson he learned in his early years in business:

"Years ago when I was very young," he recalls, "a VP of Hyatt looked at me and said, 'You look, but you don't see.' I learned to look not just at the big picture, but also at every place setting, light fixture, and customer exchange. See every crack, every detail. I learned to really see and not just look at my business."

When you stay tuned into your business and are aware of your surroundings, you'll better anticipate the need for change and adjustment and be able to quickly pivot and adapt when the time comes.

Growth isn't a straight line to the top it's more like scaling a rock wall. It's a slow, steady, strategic climb, and you need to be aware of every handhold, foothold, and loose stone in order to make it to the summit.

THERE ARE NO SHORTCUTS IN SCALING

As your business begins to grow, you may be tempted to make cuts and take shortcuts in order to reach your next goal faster. There's no more sure fire way to cripple your business, than to cut corners and try to take the easy path to success.

Every action you take now has repercussions later.

Entrepreneur and career analyst Dan Pink puts shortcuts into perspective, explaining how focusing too heavily on your end goal of scaling your business can impact your business.

"The problem with making an extrinsic reward the only destination that matters is that some people will choose the quickest route there, even if it means taking the low road. Indeed, most of the scandals and misbehaviour that have seemed endemic to modern life involve shortcuts."

When you take shortcuts, you make compromises. You compromise your ethics, your values, and the integrity of your business often at the expense of the customer and your employees.

Dallas Mavericks owner and Shark Tank host Mark Cuban remembers the best advice about success in business that he ever received:

"Do the work," says Cuban. "Out-work. Out-think. Out-sell your expectations. There are no shortcuts. My dad told me that when I was in high school. My dad did upholstery on cars, and he was always very encouraging, but also realistic."

CHAPTER 5

RISKS THAT COME FROM SCALING YOUR BUSINESS

So you've launched a business and you've gotten a taste of success; you're thinking you may be ready to start scaling up, taking your business to the next level and driving revenue through the roof. But as you grow, your resources and investment has to scale proportionately, and you need to ensure your infrastructure and organizational systems can handle the scaling. If you aren't adequately prepared for the scaling up process, you could risk your entire business. Consider the following risks that are associated with business growth before initiating any measures to scale your startup.

1. YOU'LL WORK LONG HOURS

Many entrepreneurs struggle to find work-life balance, and if you're already feeling the weight of the enormous amount of time, effort, and energy it takes to generate and sustain business, remember that it will take just as much work to scale up every step of the way. Growth doesn't happen overnight, so you're bound to be working overtime for quite some time, before you start seeing results from all that investment; even hiring an entire team to help you out, won't get you off the hook for giving it all you've got to grow bigger and better.

2. YOUR EXISTING CUSTOMERS MAY FEEL ALIENATED

In order to scale your business, it's going to be necessary for you to divert a lot of time, attention, and resources to growing your audience, exploring new markets, and attracting new customers. Chances are good, that your loyal customers, the ones that have brought you all your success in the first place, have come to expect a certain level of customer service, and they may be frustrated by changes associated with growth. Especially if your business's scaling means developing new products, existing customers may worry they'll miss out on the original draws your business offered.

3. YOU MAY BE CAUGHT IN THE TIDE

According to Entrepreneur, "many rapidly growing businesses get burned by investing in more capacity and taking on higher fixed expenses, not realizing that their growth may be a temporary thing." As the old saying goes, it's critical that you don't put the cart before the horse; make sure you've got a solid system for predicting demand, sales, and trends and that you have a plan for adjusting both fixed and variable expenses to stay profitable regardless of market fluctuations. Of course, it's not really about being able to predict the future; it's really just about having flexibility built into your business plan to protect yourself should you find yourself caught in a tidal market.

4. YOU MAY EXPOSE YOURSELF TO LEGAL ISSUES

Scaling up usually necessitates hiring more employees, which opens the door for human resources related legal issues. Depending on the number of people you employ, you may be legally required to offer health insurance and other benefits, and laws vary widely regarding hours of work, breaks, downsizing and layoffs, and other employment rights issues. As your business grows, it will become more and more necessary to understand how the employment law system works to protect yourself, your employees, and your business.

5. YOU MAY HAVE TO LOOSEN THE REIGNS

If you built your company from the ground up, it may be a real challenge to accept the fact that the management and leadership structures, that worked well for your team of 25, doesn't work quite so well now that you've grown to a staff of 250. Scaling up brings challenges, that may require adaptations to your leadership structure, up to and including loosening the reigns on your business and delegating tasks to people more qualified than yourself in specific areas.

6. YOU'LL EVENTUALLY HAVE TO TRIM THE FAT

Too many entrepreneurs make the mistake of believing growth means upward, outward, bigger, and more. In reality, scaling means outgrowing, shifting, and changing things up. That means you may find strategies, that no longer work, departments, which are no longer efficient, and even staff members, who don't fit the company culture or cause unnecessary setbacks and controversies. Accepting, that not everything will work and that sometimes you'll have to cut ties, will help your company transform.

7. YOU MAY BE AT INCREASED RISK FOR CYBERCRIME

Growth can be a double-edged sword, when it comes to cyber security, since more employees means more potential avenues for hacker infiltration. Moreover, hackers are naturally more attracted to more successful enterprises. A 2016 Ponemon Institute report found, that employee negligence was the top concern for more than half (53 percent) of businesses as it relates to data breaches. If you don't find ways to ingrain cyber security into your company culture, employees may accidentally expose your business to enormous risk.

IF YOU'VE BEEN DEBATING WHETHER YOU SHOULD TAKE STEPS TO SCALE YOUR BUSINESS, BE SURE YOU'VE MITIGATED THE POTENTIAL RISKS OF DOING SO AS MUCH AS POSSIBLE

BEFORE INVESTING THE TIME, ENERGY, AND MONEY IT WILL TAKE TO GROW.

CHAPTER 6

BIGGEST RISKS OF SCALING UP

Which of these 5 potentially fatal scaling mistakes is your company making?

If 20 years of coaching business owners to scale their companies has taught me anything it is this: the overwhelming majority of entrepreneurs want growth.

They focus on it; work towards it; and even obsess over it.

But sometimes scaling up your company can put you at risk.

Here are the five biggest risks I've observed from working with hundreds of businesscoaching clients as they scaled their companies.

RISK #1: CASH FLOW CHALLENGES

Generally, growth costs cash, and that cash often is needed in advance of added revenues.

For example, one of the manufactures we've been coaching for seven years now, estimates it costs them roughly $400,000-500,000 in startup costs to begin to make a new contract manufacturing part family. These costs are engineering time, C&C programing costs, tooling and machine costs, all of which occur before any new part comes off of production.

Then they have a 90-day lag between the time they buy the raw materials, produce, and actually ship their first parts, and the time they actually receive payment for those parts.

But their contracts are lucrative and typically run five years, so they want to grow more of them, but they need the capital to do so. For them they both self-finance some of this and tap as needed into a business line of credit.

This imbalance of cash flow is the most straightforward kind. But it often comes in more dangerous variations.

For example, in one service business I owned, we had over $125,000 per month of excess payroll, that we didn't shed for close to 10 months.

One of the most important things you can do, to protect yourself, if you are growing fast is to keep a 90-120 rolling cash flow projection that you watch weekly to keep a close eye on your cash flow.

RISK #2: GETTING CAUGHT IN A "TIDAL" MARKET

The tide comes in; the tide goes out. Many rapidly growing businesses get burned by investing in more capacity and taking on higher fixed expenses, not realizing, that their growth may be a temporarily thing.

I shared above about my past company's cash flow challenge with excess staffing. What caused that, was four years of 100 percent growth per year, colouring my decision making glasses. I didn't look at the market data, that would have shown me, that that growth rate was likely to taper off. Instead, I invested heavily on scaling up our staff to handle the projected growth. Not only did that growth slow, but in fact, for a year period we had a decline in sales. That was a $1 millions of lost profit lesson that I won't soon repeat.

How can you get better and better at predicting demand and sales? What are the clues that might indicate that your sales volume or margins might take a hit? By reviewing these factors quarterly, you stay clear on how to adjust your fixed and variable expenses to stay profitable regardless of the market demand.

Also, how can you build flexibility into your expenses to be able to quickly dial back your non-strategic costs, should the situation warrant it? Could you go with a shorter term lease with "options to renew"? Could you build a 60-day escape clause into a key vendor contract, if you need to get out of it? Could you lease overflow staffing versus hirer more employees yourself? You get the idea. A little judicious negotiating a contract time can go a long way, to protect you should you be caught in a tidal market.

RISK #3: LOSS OF FOCUS

This is one of the most prevalent risks of fast growth, that I see in our business coaching clients. They are so attracted to a new opportunity (e.g. a new market, new sales channel, new product line, etc.), that they pull their attention away from what matters most to their business.

This is so common we even have a name for it - "Bright Shiny Object Syndrome."

Have you ever been guilty of Bright Shiny Object Syndrome?

How do you protect yourself from it and keep your best resources on your best opportunities?

First, do your strategic planning quarterly, following a defined, structured process. If you are tempted by a luring opportunity mid-quarter, be cautious about going after it. Most of the clients we coach are really good about resist poor temptations when they do their formal planning, but struggle most, when the opportunity comes "out of nowhere" during their normal workday. At this point they shortcut their structured planning discipline and make emotional decisions, that lead them down the wrong path. Once committed, they rarely revisit these decisions, even years after the choice has proven to be a real waste.

For example, one software company we coach frittered away several hundred thousands of dollars of profits over a 24-month period chasing oversees sales of its industry dominant software. They could have grown by two or three-fold more than they did in this period, if they had not spread their attention over too broad a front. The initial decision came mid-quarter, and in fact, they only told us about the decision after they had already sunk significant resources about it to open up two foreign sales offices.

Second, get outside perspective to both challenge your allocation of resources and to hold you accountable to your decisions. This could be a formal business coach, or an informal board of advisors. The key is you need this to be from an outside party, who won't be afraid to call you on your behaviour. It's hard for your staff to challenge you, after all there is a real power imbalance. But the right coach or advisor will be able to do this for you.

RISK #4: LOSS OF "COHERENCE".

Coherence means the core parts of your business all being aligned and in sync with one another, supporting and reinforcing each other. Too many fast growing companies lose their coherence as they scale. They slap together solutions and strategies, that don't fit together, and in fact may work against themselves.

RISK #5: CALLING ATTENTION TO A LUCRATIVE MARKET NICHE, THAT YOU CAN'T SATISFY FAST ENOUGH

In biology they say, that an unfilled ecological niche is ripe for a new entrant to rapidly take over.

In business, if you bring to light a new, high margin, low competition market niche, and then don't have the sales or production capability to satiate that market demand fast enough, some other company will come in and fill that empty market niche.

This is why platform tech companies work so hard to get to scale quickly, even at the cost of tens or even hundreds of millions of dollars. They know that if the market is big enough and profitable enough, someone else is going to get their soon unless they dominate the space fast enough. Just look at Uber, airbnd, and priceline.com. They all invested heavily to get to scale fast enough to sell and fulfil on the market demand for their niche.

SIGNS YOU'RE SCALING YOUR COMPANY TOO QUICKLY

When your company is in growth mode, you might feel empowered by the exciting changes you're bringing to your organization. You're hiring new people, launching new campaigns and building new partnerships you're on top of the world, and you feel like nothing can slow you down.

While it's good to be motivated when you're scaling up, there is such a thing as growing too quickly. When the adrenaline wears off, you might realize, that you've hired or spent prematurely, leaving your business in a very difficult position.

1. **Growth Is Breaking The Foundation Of Your Business**

Growth is a good thing, but not at the expense of your foundation breaking down. Can capital keep up with the growth? Are your people leading the change? Is the culture being sacrificed or transforming with the growth? Are your "base business" customers still happy? All of these questions are critical and serve as stop gates for your organization when scaling.

2. You Don't Have The Right New Hire To New Business Ratio

If companies get funding, the first thing they do is to hire people to innovate. Investors care about you maintaining a responsible business no matter, what size you are or what size you scale to. If you're hiring ahead of the work and the work doesn't come through, that's a problem. Your eye on operations and its relationship to new business is absolutely key to growing in a smart way.

3. You're Getting A Lot Of Complaints

A huge giveaway that you are scaling too fast is complaints from those you serve. Ensure you make it very easy for a customer to complain. If you are never made aware of mounting complaints, you may see the results reflected in diminishing revenues. So, listen to complaints from customers. They will guide you where you need to put your focus and where you need to fix underlying problems.

4. You're Dropping the Ball Where You Used to Perform Well

It isn't unusual for leadership teams to stumble in areas they had previously "mastered." Maintaining products, clients and services, that served as the foundation for growth, are often sacrificed to make space for future focus. A mindful organization will avoid this misstep by establishing strong operational rhythms and scorecards, that they keep in front of employees at all levels of the company.

5. You're Noticing Big Cash Flow Gaps

Having significant demand can also mean an increase in costs to meet that demand. If you can't fund the demand until invoices are paid, a cash gap will quickly emerge. This puts pressure on covering your own businesses expenses and can create reputational risk in the market. Fiercely manage your cash flow. If you can't fund it, don't do it until you have identified the solutions to fill the gaps.

6. You and Your Staff Can't Keep Up

A sign that your company is scaling too fast is, that you and your staff are spread thin. This can manifest in poor customer service, tasks falling through the cracks from a lack of follow-up, slow product or service delivery, and not having time to train or implement systems. A solution is pulling back on marketing and sales temporarily, to get a handle on the current volume and problem areas.

7. Your Staff Members Are Becoming Workaholics

If an entrepreneur or CEO is scaling their company too quickly, stress, workaholics and poor performance will set in. This is a sign, that the process needs to be slowed down, and more thought, time, patience and cultivation of company culture will be required to be truly successful. When a company scales too quickly, workers may start cutting corners to meet demands, which can result in disaster.

8. You're No Longer Delivering Value

When a company scales too quickly and doesn't have the structure to support the growth, failure rates will increase. If you fail to deliver value, you'll lose wallet share. As you lose wallet share, your failure rate will increase as you struggle. To ensure you don't become obsolete, focus on your core deliverables first. When you have those items fully upright, then press into growth activities.

9. You're Not Living Out Your Core Values

Sometimes we are so focused on the bottom line and expansion, that we lose sight of purpose and quality of life. If we are not living our core values and from a place of integrity, it could be, that we've lost sight of our purpose. The antidote? Revisit core values. Get feedback from a trusted friend, coach or mentor. Review, reset and replan.

CHAPTER 7

OPPORTUNITIES TO SCALE YOUR BUSINESS WITH DATA

Almost across the board, businesses are asking themselves:

"How are we going to grow our business to the next stage?"

No matter what industry you are in, using your company's data is imperative to understanding how to scale, and at what pace. We'll look at ways that data can be leveraged to turbocharge your business scaling strategy.

So now you have "big data".

"Big data" was traditionally the term for data sets, that were too complex for traditional data-processing applications to deal with. Today, we have access to tons of data, and the means to process and analyze it. That begs the question, what's next? Here are 3 tips on how to tap your data to scale your business successfully.

1: IMPROVE PRODUCTIVITY

The correct use of data can be one of the key drivers to increase productivity. This can be in in terms of boosting output, or being more efficient including ensuring that the right people are focused on the right tasks. Better data integration across a range of internal and external sources can cut down on search times and help analysts, auditors, and others spend less time tracking down information and more time applying the results. Professionals can run the numbers on much bigger sets of data, do better vetting, and do it all faster, allowing specialists to apply their skills in other ways.

While AI and machine-learning tools do require a more significant investment of time and resources, many other capabilities can be created using tools and systems, that most organizations have in place today, and then refine from there.

Data can uncover areas where productivity can be improved: whether it's production levels at a manufacturing plant, or the numbers of a nationwide sales team, failing to leverage business data in order to scale is a huge missed opportunity.

2: INCREASE OPPORTUNITIES

Research suggests that companies effectively leveraging customer behavioural insights will outperform peers by 25% in terms of gross margin, and an incredible 85% in sales growth. Such insights are driven by data.

For some businesses, it can be as simple as stocking certain products together. For others, it may be insights into the buyer's journey, effective retargeting, or appealing to the customer at exactly the right time and place.

Many of these trends, patterns, and opportunities would not be available, if it wasn't for the ability to query large amounts of data. Now, big data analytics tools can uncover these opportunities. While some of these could be uncovered anecdotally for example a sales person noticing, that people buying a certain shirt would often buy a specific belt, this is certainly not scalable.

For uncovering scalability opportunities, and using them to scale your business, data is key.

3: REDUCE BOTTLENECKS

Most organizations experience bottlenecks of some kind; a process or part thereof which holds things back and, if this bottleneck is eliminated, will result in increased efficiency for the organization.

The "traditional" bottleneck is found in a manufacturing environment. For example, an auto part might have to be galvanized. The process may take time, as only a certain amount of parts can be galvanized per hour. This leads to a build-up of parts at this point in the process, and a bottleneck ensues.

Bottlenecks can be found in any part of the business however; from transport and logistics, to approvals and technology. Data is critical in identifying, and solving these bottlenecks and restoring efficiency to the organization.

Today in a manufacturing environment for example, data can be analyze to predict bottlenecks, prevent overstock, and manage situations where certain orders spike. The same applies to any area of business, where the power of data used correctly can streamline process, remove bottlenecks even before they occur, and ensure scalable success for organizations.

CHAPTER 8

CONCLUSION

Congratulations again!

You have accomplished a step; most business owners never master. You gained a fast amount of knowledge, which now enables you to lift your business to the next level:

- You know what business scalability means.

- You learnt the difference between normal growth and upscaling.

- You understand the busniss fundings, that will scale your business and you even gained a five step instruction to adapt the fundings to your own business.

- You know the importance of the SOUL for your business.

- You benefit from the success stories of other entrepreneurs and you are able to transfer them to your own business.

- You got to know the risks of scaling and even more important the signs, when your business is scaling too fast.

- You learnt how to us big data, to easily scale your business.

Finally, I have one more advise for you:

Don't just read this book once and never look at it again. The topic of business scalabilty is complex and you might need to repeat the individual chapters a few times. That is not a sign of dullness, but much rather shows your willingness to completetly commit yourself to this extremely successful business topic.

I wish you all the best for yourself and your business.

DID YOU ENJOY MY BOOK?

Now you have read my book, you know how best to scale your busines. This is why I am asking you now for a small favour. Customer reviews are an important part of every product offered by Amazon. It is the first thing that customers look at and, more often than not, is the main reason whether or not they decide to buy the product. Considering the endless number of products available at Amazon, this factor is becoming increasingly important.

If you liked my book, I would be more than grateful if you could leave your review by Amazon. How do you do that? Just click on the "Write a customer review"-button (as shown below), which you find on the Amazon product page of my book or your orders site:

Review this product

Share your thoughts with other customers

Just write a short review as to whether you particularly liked my book or if there is something I can improve on. It will not take more than 2 minutes, honestly!

Be assured, I will read every review personally. It will help me a lot to improve my books and to tailor them to your wishes.

For this I say to you:

Thank you very much!

Yours

James

LIST OF REFERENCES:

Bondi, André B. (2000). Characteristics of scalability and their impact on performance. Proceedings of the second international workshop on Software and performance – WOSP '00.
p. 195. *doi*:*10.1145/350391.350432*. *ISBN* *15811 3195X*.

Hill, Mark D. (1990). "What is scalability?". ACM SIGARCH Computer Architecture News. **18** (4): 18. *doi*:*10.1145/121973.121975*.

Duboc, Leticia; Rosenblum, David S.; Wicks, Tony (2006). A framework for modelling and analysis of software systems scalability. Proceedings of the 28th international conference on Software engineering – ICSE '06.

p. 949. _doi_:_10.1145/1134285.1134460_. _ISBN_ _159 5933751_.

Laudon, Kenneth Craig; Traver, Carol Guercio (2008). _E-commerce: Business, Technology, Society_. Pearson Prentice Hall/Pearson Education. _ISBN_ _9780136006459_.

Hesham El-Rewini and Mostafa Abd-El-Barr (April 2005). _Advanced Computer Architecture and Parallel Processing_. _John Wiley & Sons_. p. 66. _ISBN_ _978-0-471-47839-3_.

Michael, Maged; Moreira, Jose E.; Shiloach, Doron; Wisniewski, Robert W. (March 26, 2007). _Scale-up x Scale-out: A Case Study using Nutch/Lucene_. 2007 IEEE International Parallel and Distributed Processing Symposium. p. 1. _doi_:_10.1109/IPDPS.2007.370631_. _ISBN_ _1-4244-0909-8_.

"Network Functions Virtualisation (NFV); Terminology for Main Concepts in NFV" (PDF).

Base One (2007). _"Database Scalability - Dispelling myths about the limits of database-centric architecture"_. Retrieved May 23, 2007.

Google (2018). _"Choosing a storage option"_. Retrieved January 24, 2018.

"Spanner: Google's Globally-Distributed Database" (PDF). OSDI'12 Proceedings of the 10th USENIX conference on Operating Systems Design and Implementation. 2012: 251–264. _ISBN_ _978-1-931971-96-6_.
Retrieved September 30, 2012.

Sadek Drobi (January 11, 2008). _"Eventual consistency by Werner Vogels"_. InfoQ. Retrieved April 8, 2017.

"The Weak Scaling of DL POLY 3". STFC Computational Science and Engineering Department. Archived from *the original* on March 7, 2014. Retrieved March 8, 2014.

DISCLAIMER

Printed in Great Britain
by Amazon